Bad Dog, Growly!

by Pippa Goodhart   illustrated by Steve Stone

OXFORD
UNIVERSITY PRESS
AUSTRALIA & NEW ZEALAND

OXFORD
UNIVERSITY PRESS

Oxford University Press is a department of the University of Oxford.
It furthers the University's objective of excellence in research, scholarship,
and education by publishing worldwide. Oxford is a registered trademark
of Oxford University Press in the UK and in certain other countries.

Published in Australia by
Oxford University Press
Level 8, 737 Bourke Street, Docklands, Victoria 3008, Australia

Text © Pippa Goodhart 2015, 2019

The moral rights of the author have been asserted.

First published 2015
This edition 2019
Reprinted 2021 (twice)

ISBN 9780190316952

Series Advisor: Nikki Gamble
Designed by Kim Ferguson
Illustrated by Steve Stone
Printed in China by Leo Paper Products Ltd

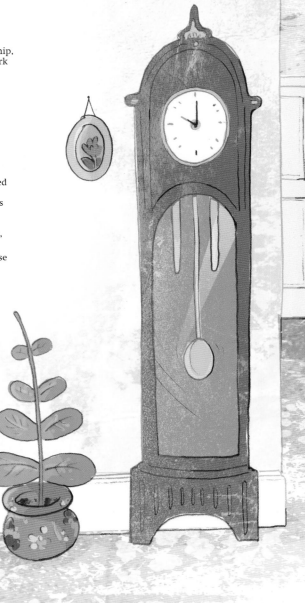

Growly had a big mouth, big teeth and a *big* growl.

"**Growl!**"

Growly was a bad, *bad* dog. Everybody said so.
Even Miss Petal said that Growly was a bad dog.
Growly was her dog, so she should know.

Miss Poppy Petal was a sweet, *sweet* old lady. Everybody said so. They said that Growly was lucky to live with her.

4

One day, Miss Petal said, "We're going to the shops for some apples."

"**Growl**," said Growly.

"Hurry up, you bad dog," said Miss Petal. And off they went down the road.

"Good morning, Miss Petal," said a man in a hat.

"Good morning," said Miss Petal sweetly. "I am going to get some apples to make a lovely apple pie."

"That's nice," said the man in the hat.

"What a sweet little boy!" said Miss Petal to a lady with a pusher. She bent down to pat the little boy on his head. But then ...

"Cough, cough!" went Miss Petal loudly,
turning around so no one could see her.

"Waaaaa!" cried the little boy.
Somebody had taken his ice cream!
Who would steal an ice cream from a child?

"**Growl!**" went Growly.

Miss Petal and Growly went further along the road.
They came to a lady in a pink coat.

"What a lovely dog you have," said Miss Petal sweetly.

"Oh, thank you!" said the lady in the pink coat.
"She's my poodle, Lulu."

A man with some apples was walking down the road.

"**Growl!**"

went Growly.

And then ...

The man dropped his apples all over the road!
But who tripped him up?

"It must have been your dog!" said the lady in the pink coat. "I feel sorry for you, Miss Petal. You have such a bad, *bad* dog."

"Bad dog, Growly!" said Miss Petal. And she helped the man pick up his apples.

"Growl!" went Growly.

13

Then Miss Petal and Growly went to get some fish. When they got to the fish shop, Miss Petal tied Growly's lead to a post. Lulu the lovely dog was there, too.

"Yap, yap, yap!" went Lulu. She was very upset.

"**Growl!**" went Growly.

"Who could have upset that lovely little dog?"
said an old man with a walking frame.
"It must have been that bad dog."

"Bad dog, Growly!" said Miss Petal.

But then …

15

"**Howl!**" went Growly really loudly.

Big Alf from the fish shop and the lady in the pink coat ran outside.

"Oh!" gasped the lady in the pink coat. "Where's my little Lulu? That bad dog, Growly, must have *eaten* her!"

But Big Alf said, "Look! There's your Lulu – and there's the bad woman who took her!"

"Good dog, Growly!" said Big Alf. "You howled to warn us! Would you like to live with me instead of that nasty Miss Petal?"

"**Growl**," went Growly softly, and he wagged his tail.

"Good," said Big Alf. "Let's go on a picnic."

Big Alf closed his shop. He and Growly
went for a walk, and then they had a picnic.
Growly carried the basket.

wag

wag

wag

"You're a *good* dog, Growly," said Big Alf.

Growly and Big Alf went home. Big Alf
did the dishes and Growly cleaned the
crumbs off the floor.

"Good dog, Growly," said Big Alf.

"Growl!" said Growly.

Growly and Big Alf lived happily ever after ...

... but Miss Poppy Petal did not!